POP BUCHANAN

ChatGPT Writing Secrets

How to Humanize Your Writing, Keep Your Voice, Avoid AI Robotic Signatures, and Em Dashes

First edition

This book was professionally typeset on Reedsy.
Find out more at reedsy.com

Contents

Preface

Author's Integrity Statement

(A Note on Authorship, Technology, and the Future of Writing)

This book was written to protect the human voice in a world that is changing faster than ever. As artificial intelligence becomes part of the creative process, we face an important question: how do we use new tools without losing what makes us human?

ChatGPT Writing Secrets is not a product of automation. It is a product of collaboration. Every word, idea, and story was guided, refined, and approved by the human author, Pop Buchanan. Artificial intelligence was used only for editorial support, organization, and research verification. The heart and meaning of every sentence remain fully human.

At Pop Buchanan & Company, every book and project, whether Sober Is Dope, The Sober Brain Reset, or Invest AI, comes from a place of truth, love, and lived experience. We believe writing is both an art and a service.

This book was written to prepare writers for the next chapter

of human creativity. Over the coming decade, AI will likely become as common in writing as word processors or spell checkers. The goal is not to fight that future but to enter it with integrity. Writers must learn how to guide these tools, to shape them, and to use them in ways that amplify their truth instead of replacing it.

ChatGPT Writing Secrets exists to serve as a foundation for this new era. It teaches how to stay accurate, human, and honest. It teaches how to keep your name, your voice, and your ideas clear in a digital world where shortcuts are easy and authenticity is rare.

To every writer who reads this book: do not fear technology. Master it. Use it as an ally, not as a disguise. Let it lift your craft, not replace your effort. True creativity does not come from prediction or code. It comes from heart, memory, and courage.

Pop Buchanan and all works published under his name stand for those values. We are proud to use AI responsibly, transparently, and with purpose. The future of writing belongs to those who create with integrity and share their truth with the world.

Writing is the heartbeat of human connection. It carries our thoughts, memories, and imagination through time. Yet, we live in a moment where technology is learning to write alongside us. Every day, we see more stories, articles, and books that sound the same, as if they were all written by one digital ghost.

I remember how long it took me to finish my first book, Sober

Is Dope. Three years of writing, editing, rewriting, and waiting. There were mistakes. There were doubts. But every word was mine. I knew every sentence had passed through my heart before it reached the page. That experience made me realize what is worth protecting.

When ChatGPT appeared, I saw something incredible. It was not a threat to writers but a powerful assistant. It could help edit, organize, and research faster than ever. Yet I also saw how easy it was for people to lose themselves in the process. A person could ask for a chapter, get a page of text, and think the work was done. That kind of writing feels empty because it misses what makes us human: the struggle, the emotion, and the choice of every word.

This book is a reminder that you are the writer. ChatGPT and other AI models are tools. They can polish, shape, and speed up your work, but they cannot replace your voice. ChatGPT Writing Secrets exists to help people rediscover their creative control in an age when so many are letting machines speak for them.

You will learn how to write with clarity, how to stay accurate, how to sound human, and how to stop the small habits that give away robotic text, such as the overuse of em dashes or the shallow rhythm of AI-style sentences. Most of all, you will learn how to write with your own truth again.

This book is my open letter to creators everywhere. We do not need to fear AI. We need to master it with ethics, creativity, and purpose. If you have ever looked at your work and thought,

"This does not sound like me anymore," this book will help you bring your voice back.

Introduction

Why I Wrote ChatGPT Writing Secrets

I wrote ChatGPT Writing Secrets to give people something the internet desperately needs: a path back to authentic, human-centered writing in a digital world. Everywhere I look, I see AI signatures creeping into journalism, creative projects, and even classrooms. The future of writing will not belong to humans or machines alone. It will be a mix of both. The question is, who will control that partnership? Will it be you, or the machine?

This book is not about replacing writers or giving people shortcuts. It is about protecting the craft of writing from automation that has no thought, feeling, or soul. My goal is to help people use tools like ChatGPT as skilled editorial and research partners, not as ghostwriters. When used with discipline, AI can make the editing process faster, cleaner, and more organized. But when used without care or creativity, it drains the art out of the work.

I do not support plagiarism or lazy writing. I do not encourage anyone to hand in AI-generated work as their own. Writing has always been about effort, research, and personal reflection. What I encourage instead is balance: your voice, your ideas, and your structure first, then AI as a technical assistant that helps refine your vision. When you outline your story, define your message, and let AI assist with editing and organization, you are not cheating. You are collaborating intelligently and saving time while keeping your integrity.

The problem begins when people skip that process. When they let AI write from nothing, something sacred is lost. The result is what I call synthetic writing, which looks perfect on the surface but feels hollow underneath. It sounds smooth, but it lacks pulse. It reads like information, not inspiration. That is what this book aims to change.

Technology can be a gift when used with wisdom. It can remove years of tedious editing from a book project. It can help people find clarity in complex ideas. But it can never feel what you feel. It cannot capture heartbreak, joy, or wonder. It cannot replace the part of writing that comes from lived experience and deep thought. Without a human voice, writing becomes lifeless and repetitive. With direction and purpose, however, AI becomes a faithful assistant that helps bring your message to life.

That is why I created the Universal Writing Rules that shape this book. These rules help writers stay consistent, protect credibility, organize complex ideas, and sound genuinely human. They remove the habits that give away robotic text, such as overusing em dashes, copying phrasing patterns, or letting rhythm fall flat. They also keep language simple and clear so that anyone can understand your message, no matter their background or level of education.

ChatGPT Writing Secrets is not here to flood the world with more content. It exists to bring care, emotion, and originality back into the writing process. Whether you are a teacher, student, artist, or entrepreneur, this book will help you think deeper, write faster, and sound like your true self again.

PRO TIP: *Why You Need the Pro Plan to Unlock ChatGPT Writing Secrets*

To use the systems in this book fully, you need ChatGPT Pro. The free plan is fine for testing ideas, but it forgets your work, limits your files, and blocks tools like document uploads, memory, and image creation. The Pro Plan gives you the full studio, fast reasoning, long-term memory, unlimited revisions, and access to specialized GPTs for writing, editing, and art. If you are building books, scripts, or long projects, this upgrade is not a luxury. It is the key that makes every method in this book work the way it was designed to.

1

Meet Your New Writing Partner

Writing has always been a conversation between the mind and the page. Now a new partner has joined that conversation. It does not sleep, forget (Well... Sometimes forget LOL), or get tired. It is fast, curious, and sometimes too confident. Its name is ChatGPT.

ChatGPT is not a ghostwriter, a thinker, or a rival. It is a pattern reader. It studies billions of examples of language and predicts what words come next. When you ask it for a story, an outline, or an idea, it gives you its best guess of what words should follow each other. That prediction can feel like magic, but it is only the reflection of all the human words it has already seen.

Your job as a writer is to guide that reflection so that it points back to your own voice. Think of AI as a mirror that needs direction. When you shape the question, build the outline, and describe the tone, you are programming your reflection. Without that human steering wheel, the mirror repeats what it already knows, and the result sounds flat and mechanical.

Many writers begin by asking AI to write a full chapter or essay from nothing. That is where things go wrong. The result may look perfect on the surface, but it will read like a copy of a copy. It has rhythm but no heartbeat. It says the right words but not the right truth. Good writing still begins with you. Your experiences, your struggles, and your sense of rhythm make your work real.

A better way is to start with an outline of your own. Write down the points you want to make, the feeling you want the reader to have, and the message that matters most. Then use ChatGPT as your assistant. Ask it to help you brainstorm ideas, find structure, or expand your notes into full paragraphs. Let it clean the grammar while you protect the meaning. Use it to check facts, but always verify them with your own research. When you stay in control, the technology saves you time without stealing your style.

Remember that tools can help polish a diamond, but they cannot make one. ChatGPT can smooth your sentences, catch errors, and suggest better phrasing, but the sparkle must come from you. If you feed it lazy prompts, you get lazy results. If you bring strong ideas and clear direction, you get work that shines.

To keep your writing natural, read your words aloud. Your ear will notice what your eyes miss. If it sounds robotic, fix the rhythm. Replace vague words with ones that describe what you actually see or feel. Keep sentences short and specific. If a line sounds like something the internet could have written, it needs more of you in it.

The best writers of this new era will not be the ones who type the fastest. They will be the ones who know how to make AI listen. They will blend heart with structure and turn machine assistance into human advantage. ChatGPT Writing Secrets will show you how to do exactly that.

Your new writing partner is powerful, but it needs a leader. Be that leader. Guide the conversation. Protect your tone. Trust your instinct more than the algorithm. When you learn to work with AI as an assistant instead of a replacement, you will write faster, smarter, and more honestly than ever before.

2

The ChatGPT Modes: Your Creative Switchboard

Every writer needs a system. Painters have palettes, musicians have scales, and writers now have modes. Modes are simple settings you can turn on and off in your process to stay organized, clear, and in control. When you learn to use them, you stop guessing how to guide your writing and start leading it.

Think of the modes as switches on a creative control board. Each one helps you focus on a different part of the craft. Some protect accuracy, some build structure, and some remind you to sound like yourself. The more you practice, the faster you can flip between them as you write.

The first mode is **Accuracy Mode**. This mode keeps you honest. It asks you to check facts, confirm sources, and make sure that what you say can be proven. It means never making up statistics or quotes. When you use AI, accuracy becomes even more important, because AI can sound confident even when it is wrong. Always read with a question in mind: "How do I know this is true?" That habit will keep your credibility strong.

Next is **Objective Mode**. This mode helps you separate facts from feelings. It does not remove emotion; it balances it. Use this when you write about serious topics or when you need to explain both sides of an idea. It keeps your tone steady and your logic sound.

Then comes **Humanize Mode**. This is one of the most important switches. It brings life back into the text. In this mode you trade vague words for clear ones. You write as if you are talking to a friend instead of performing for a crowd. You use real images, short sentences, and simple rhythm. You make the reader feel that a real person is speaking. When you use AI, turn this mode on during revision. Ask yourself, "Would I say this out loud to someone I care about?" If not, rewrite it until you would.

Prose-Only Mode is next. This mode removes lists, outlines, and bullets from your final draft. Everything flows in full sentences and paragraphs. It trains you to write in a steady rhythm that sounds natural when read aloud. In this book, we use Prose-Only Mode for every chapter because we want the work to feel like a conversation, not a manual.

Reading Level Mode keeps your language clear. The best writing is not the fanciest; it is the easiest to understand. This mode reminds you to use short words, strong verbs, and one idea per sentence. It makes your work readable by anyone, anywhere.

There is also **Continuity Mode**, which helps you keep track of what you have said and what you still need to say. You keep a small file called your Canon (knowledge-based project memory tool). Inside, you store your facts, definitions, outlines, and notes. This mode stops you from repeating yourself or changing direction halfway through a project. It also protects you from the mistake of forgetting what tone or point of view you used earlier.

The final mode we will often use is **Human Ethics Mode**. This mode is your moral compass. It asks you to respect the boundary between help and replacement. Use AI for editing, research, and organization, but never to fake effort or steal credit. Writers write. AI assists.

Once you know these modes, you can combine them like tools in a workshop. For example, when you draft, turn on Humanize Mode and Reading Level Mode. When you edit, add Accuracy Mode. When you prepare for publishing, use Continuity and Ethics Modes together. With practice, you will switch between them without thinking.

Every effective writer has rituals. These modes are your new ritual. Before you start a session, pause and decide which ones you need. Tell yourself, "Accuracy on. Humanize on. Reading Level on." That small act will focus your mind and remind you who is really in charge of your words.

The point of the modes is not to limit you. They exist to give you structure so you can create freely without getting lost. Once they become a habit, you will notice how much clearer and faster your writing feels. You will stop producing text that sounds like the machine and start producing writing that sounds like a person who knows what they mean.

You are now the one at the control panel. You decide which switch to flip, which tone to use, and which truth to tell. Master these modes, and you will never again wonder how to start or where to go next. Your writing will follow your intention, not the algorithm.

3

The Signature Writing Protocol

Every writer needs a method. Without one, you risk drifting between ideas, losing focus, and forgetting why you started writing in the first place. The Signature Writing Protocol is your anchor. It is the process that keeps your creativity alive while giving you a clear path from thought to finished work.

I created this method while struggling through my first major book. It took me years to finish, and I learned the hard way that creativity alone is not enough. I needed discipline, structure, and a way to keep my ideas in line without losing their soul. The Signature Writing Protocol was born from that experience. It gives you a way to work faster without losing your voice.

The protocol begins with **Intent Lock**. This is where you decide exactly what you want to say and why it matters. Before you write, ask yourself two questions. What is the message? Who needs to hear it? Write your answers in one clear sentence. This is your promise to the reader. It will guide every paragraph that follows. When you feel lost, come back to that line. It will remind you what the story is really about.

Next comes the **Signature Outline**. This is not a rigid list of points but a flexible map that helps you stay organized. Start with the hook. What will pull the reader in? Then write a short paragraph that explains your main idea. Follow with three to seven supporting points. These can be facts, examples, or lessons. End with a closing statement that returns to your main idea. The outline helps you plan your direction without boxing you in. You can always adjust it later, but having a guide will save you from wandering in circles.

After you outline, run a **Diversity Pass.** This step is simple but powerful. You create five versions of your opening or main idea. Each version should sound different. Maybe one is emotional, one is factual, one is poetic, one is conversational, and one is short and bold. Read all five out loud. Notice which one feels most alive. That is your best starting point. The Diversity Pass helps you explore creative directions before you commit to one. It stops you from settling for your first draft, which is almost never your best draft.

Once you pick your strongest idea, move to **Synthesis Mode**. This means blending the best parts from each version into one smooth piece of writing. You might take the tone from one version, the structure from another, and a strong phrase from a third. Combine them into a single draft that feels balanced and true to your voice.

After that, enter Prose-Only Mode. This is where you write in full paragraphs, not lists or outlines. You let your thoughts flow in sentences that connect naturally. It is okay to write too much during this stage. You can cut and polish later. The goal here is movement, not perfection.

When your first draft is done, activate **Accuracy Mode**. Check every fact, date, and reference. Make sure your sources are real and your claims can be verified. Accuracy builds trust with your reader. It also keeps you from making mistakes that AI tools might insert. Remember that ChatGPT predicts text; it does not always confirm truth. You are the one responsible for the truth.

The next step is **Continuity Mode**. Read your work from start to finish. Ask yourself if the tone, point of view, and pace stay consistent. If the energy drops, mark the spot and fix it. If a line sounds robotic or off, rewrite it in your natural voice. Keep a Canon File saved as a Doc file and stored in the K Base or the ChatGPT Knowledge base, nearby to store notes about your decisions, facts, and tone. This will keep your projects aligned over time.

Finally, end with **Humanize Mode.** This is where you polish your work until it sounds like you. Read it aloud and listen for rhythm. Replace long words with short ones if they say the same thing. Cut anything that feels cold or distant. Your goal is warmth, not decoration. Good writing is not about sounding smart; it is about sounding real.

The Signature Writing Protocol gives you balance. It combines planning with freedom, logic with creativity, and discipline with heart. If you follow it each time you start a new project, you will never face a blank page with fear again. You will have a process that works, no matter the topic or format.

The best part of this method is that it adapts to every writer. Some will outline more, some will dictate, and others will rely heavily on revision. The steps remain the same, but the rhythm is yours to define. Over time, the protocol becomes second nature. You will find yourself using it automatically without needing to think about it.

This chapter marks your first real checkpoint as a writer working with AI. From now on, every chapter you create will begin with intent, move through structure, pass through diversity, and end with your human voice intact. This is how you build consistency, clarity, and authenticity in a world that often forgets what those words mean.

Your signature as a writer is not your font or your formatting. It is your rhythm, your word choice, and the way your ideas breathe. Guard that signature. Strengthen it. Let AI sharpen your edges, but never let it change your shape. That is the heart of the Signature Writing Protocol, and it will stay with you long after this book ends.

4

Use ChatGPT Dictation to Capture Your Real Voice Before Writing

Every great idea begins with a voice. Sometimes that voice is quiet and thoughtful. Other times it is loud, fast, and full of energy. The challenge is that when you start typing, the rhythm disappears. The words lose their natural emotion and flow. Dictation brings that rhythm back to life.

Dictation is one of the simplest and most powerful tools you can use with ChatGPT. It allows you to speak before you write, capturing your natural tone and expression. When you speak, you use pauses, emotion, and instinct. When you type, you often interrupt yourself with corrections. That habit can choke creativity. Speaking first frees your mind from judgment. It allows your ideas to flow naturally and without resistance.

With ChatGPT-5, dictation is built directly into the app. You do not need any external software or complicated setup. Simply open ChatGPT on your phone or desktop, tap the microphone icon at the bottom of your chat window, and start talking.

Speak as if you are telling a story to a close friend. ChatGPT will listen and transcribe your words in real time. When you finish, ask it to "clean up my dictation while keeping my tone and personality." ChatGPT will edit your text for clarity and grammar while preserving the authenticity of your voice.

Dictation keeps your writing alive. It blends your natural energy with the precision of AI editing. You bring the heart and the truth, and ChatGPT helps refine and organize it. This is how writing becomes both natural and efficient.

If you prefer, you can also record your thoughts outside of ChatGPT. Every phone, tablet, and computer has a speech-to-text option. Speak freely for a few minutes, then copy and paste your words into ChatGPT. Ask it to organize the text into clear paragraphs while keeping your original tone. This method is useful when you want flexibility, especially when you are away from your workspace.

You can use dictation for brainstorming, journaling, outlining, or full drafting. Open ChatGPT, press the microphone, and talk through your ideas for a few minutes. When you finish, ask the model to turn your spoken words into an outline or summary. Each sentence you speak becomes a building block for your next section. Over time, you will develop a personal rhythm that helps you move from inspiration to structure with ease.

Dictation is also one of the best tools for breaking writer's block. Speaking helps bypass the part of your brain that gets stuck in overthinking. It moves you from editing mode into storytelling mode. The more you talk, the more your ideas begin to connect naturally. After a few sessions, you will notice that your spoken drafts start to sound like finished pages.

Here is a simple routine to follow:

1. Choose a quiet place where you feel comfortable speaking.
2. Open ChatGPT-5 and tap the microphone icon to activate dictation.
3. Speak for five minutes about your topic. Do not stop or overthink what you are saying.
4. When you finish, ask ChatGPT, "Can you organize what I just said into clear paragraphs while keeping my tone?"
5. Read the response, make adjustments, and continue refining your ideas.

If you cannot use ChatGPT's built-in voice feature, use your phone's speech-to-text tool or a voice recorder. Paste the transcription into ChatGPT and ask it to clean it up. The result will still carry your voice because it started from your words.

Remember, dictation is not a shortcut. It is a return to your natural voice. Many great writers and thinkers, including Maya Angelou and Ernest Hemingway, understood the power of reading or speaking their words aloud. They knew that sound reveals truth. When you use dictation, you step into that same creative tradition, allowing your spoken voice to shape your written one.

The more you practice, the stronger your connection to your voice becomes. Over time, your spoken drafts will start to resemble your final versions. You will speak with purpose and clarity, and your writing will carry the same vitality and emotion.

The most important part of this process is ownership. ChatGPT is your editor, not your author. The rhythm, emotion, and message belong to you. Dictation helps you move faster and with more authenticity. It replaces the stiffness of typing with the flow of real speech.

The next time you open ChatGPT and face a blank screen, do not freeze. Speak instead. Let your voice guide you. Record your thoughts, then let ChatGPT help you shape them into clean, polished language. The fastest way to sound human is to start human. Your voice is your fingerprint as a writer. Protect it, practice it, and let it lead the way.

5

How to Create Powerful ChatGPT Outlines That Keep You Creative

In Chapter 3, you learned the Signature Writing Protocol, a complete system for staying organized and consistent while working with AI. One of its steps was outlining. This chapter expands on that step and explains how to use ChatGPT to create strong, practical outlines for any type of writing.

Every project begins with a plan. An outline is that plan. It defines your goal, saves time, and keeps your ideas organized. Without one, you risk repeating yourself or losing direction. A solid outline helps you focus on the message and finish faster.

Start with your own ideas before using ChatGPT. Write your purpose in one clear sentence. Ask yourself what you want the reader to learn or understand by the end. Once you know that, list three to seven main points that support your message. Do not worry about order yet.

Next, ask ChatGPT to organize your list into a clear structure. You can say, "Please organize these ideas into an outline for a short essay, chapter, or presentation." Review the result, then adjust it until the flow matches your thinking. You make the final decision, not the model.

Add short notes under each heading. Write what story, example, or piece of information you plan to use to support each point. If you need more ideas, ask ChatGPT for examples, but keep only what matches your own experience. The outline should reflect your knowledge, not generic text.

Each section of your outline should answer three questions:

1. What do I want to say?
2. Why does it matter?
3. What supports this point?

When you can answer all three, your outline is ready to guide a full draft.

Keep your outline flexible. As you write, new ideas may appear. Add or move sections as needed. ChatGPT can help you rearrange or combine topics quickly. The goal is clarity, not perfection.

You can also test your structure by creating a reverse outline. After writing a few pages, paste them into ChatGPT and ask, "Can you outline what I have written so far?" Compare the result to your original plan. If it does not align, adjust your draft. This is an effective way to check whether your writing stays on track.

Always lead the process. ChatGPT is a tool for organization, not a substitute for your thinking. Begin with your ideas, refine with AI assistance, and finish with your judgment.

Before you start drafting, read your outline once more. Remove weak or repetitive points and confirm that each section supports your main goal. When the structure is clear and logical, you are ready to begin writing.

An outline helps you stay efficient and consistent. It keeps your writing focused from the first sentence to the last. Use ChatGPT to improve organization, but keep full control of your ideas and direction.

6

Build ChatGPT Memory Files to Stop Hallucinations and Stay Consistent

Writers forget things when projects get big. Characters change, dates shift, tone drifts, and facts fade. ChatGPT forgets too. It is not because it does not care, but because its memory is limited. When a chat goes on too long, it starts to shorten what came before. Important details drop off. When that happens, ChatGPT begins to guess. These guesses are called hallucinations. They sound right, but they are not. The way to stop this is to build a simple memory system inside ChatGPT.

Your memory system is called the Knowledge Base, or KBase. It is where you upload files that hold your notes, outlines, or drafts. You can find the upload button by clicking the plus sign next to the message box. On the Pro plan, you can upload Word, PDF, or text files. These uploads tell ChatGPT what is true about your project. Without them, each new chat starts with no memory. With them, ChatGPT remembers what matters and stays on track.

Inside your KBase, create a small folder called "your Canon". It is your project truth. Keep these five files there:

1. Facts Ledger. List all confirmed facts, numbers, and sources.
2. Glossary. Define key names and terms so they never change.
3. Decisions Log. Write down choices about tone, focus, or wording.
4. Outline Versions. Save each outline with the date you made it.
5. Citations List. Keep every reference in the right format.

These files work like your project memory. They keep the facts straight, maintain a steady tone, and write honestly.

ChatGPT forgets because it can only see so much text at once. After a while, it drops earlier messages. When that happens, it may skip details or rewrite what you said before. This is normal. The fix is to refresh its memory often.

Here is how to keep ChatGPT current:

Step 1: Ask ChatGPT to save your work as a document file. You can say, "Please save this progress as a Word file."

Step 2: Download that file to your computer.

Step 3: Before your next session, upload that same file to the

KBase.

Step 4: Say, "Please use this file as the current version of my project."

Step 5: Repeat this process each time you finish a major part of your project, at the start, halfway through, and before final edits.

These five steps keep ChatGPT fresh and accurate. They stop the guessing that causes errors.

If ChatGPT starts repeating ideas, losing facts, or changing tone, stop and re-upload your latest outline, rules, and notes. Once you do, the chat will reset and work from the correct information again. This step alone fixes most memory and tone problems.

When people get frustrated with ChatGPT, it is almost always because of lost context, not bad behavior. The model cannot scroll through a long chat the way a person can. Feeding it your files again gives it the focus it needs to help you properly. Think of it like reminding a helper where you left off.

Keeping your KBase updated may seem small, but it makes a big difference. It saves time, builds trust, and keeps your work consistent. Each upload tells ChatGPT what matters most. Over time, this becomes second nature. You will work faster, make fewer mistakes, and keep your voice steady from start to finish.

Every writer needs stability. The Knowledge Base gives you that. Upload your files, save your progress, and re-upload often. ChatGPT will stay sharp, and your writing will stay strong from the first page to the last.

7

Spot and Eliminate ChatGPT Synthetic Writing: Fixing AI Robotic Tone in Your Work with The Human Authenticity Protocol

Sometimes I read a paragraph that looks perfect but feels empty. The grammar is fine, the rhythm even, but the life is gone. That is what I call synthetic writing. It sounds polished yet hollow, like it was built on prediction rather than emotion.

Synthetic writing has become common. Articles, posts, and even books often share the same smooth tone. Every sentence feels balanced and safe. Nothing surprises you. That is what happens when rhythm replaces pulse.

Writing with ChatGPT should never mean losing yourself. The goal is partnership, not replacement. If you understand your voice and your purpose, your work can still feel alive. The model can polish, but the feeling must come from you.

When I write, I think about how the reader will feel. I remind myself that warmth and care make a sentence human. Machines cannot fake care. That is our job.

The Problem with Perfection

AI text often sounds too clean. It flows evenly, but perfection can feel cold. Real writing bends, pauses, and shifts. It has breath. Readers might not notice the flaw in perfect rhythm, but they feel it. A few rough edges make words believable.

Small imperfections do not weaken writing. They prove that a real person was here. The point is not to create mistakes, but to leave room for rhythm and feeling.

How to Spot Synthetic Writing

When I see synthetic writing, I notice patterns. Sentences repeat the same shape: claim, example, conclusion. The flow never changes pace. The tone stays polite and cautious.

Here are the clues I look for:

Flat rhythm. Every line moves at the same speed. Break it up. Read aloud. Add a short burst after a long thought.

No emotion. It explains, but never cares. Ask, What do I want the reader to feel? Then add one real example or moment of truth.

Safe phrases. Lines like “in today’s world” or “it is important to note" belong to templates. Replace them with something specific.

Big words hiding small meaning. Simple words carry more truth. Say it plainly.

No voice. If the writing avoids "I," "you," or "we," it sounds like no one is speaking. Bring yourself back into the page.

How I Fix It

When my work feels too smooth, I use ChatGPT as a mirror. I paste my text and say, "Show me where this sounds robotic or repetitive." The model highlights patterns I might miss. Then I rewrite those lines in my own rhythm. If I did not say it aloud, I changed it.

I also turn on what I call Humanize Mode. That means replacing vague lines with vivid ones. Instead of "People face challenges," I write, "People wake up tired and stare at the ceiling before finding the will to move." Real details beat perfect sentences every time.

Another habit that helps is to underline generic words in a paragraph and swap them for precise ones. Change "thing" to "letter." Change "feel" to "ache." Change "good" to "steady." Specific words build texture, and texture builds trust.

The Six Rules of Human Authenticity

Over time, I built six simple rules that keep my writing real:

1. Vary the rhythm. Let some sentences breathe and others run.
2. Show emotion; do not explain it.
3. Take a stance. Readers respect clear conviction.
4. Avoid filler and template words.
5. Keep a little roughness. The mind trusts small imperfections.
6. Speak with certainty. Cut hedges like "perhaps" or "somewhat."

These rules are not strict; they are reminders to sound human.

Practicing Authentic Rhythm

When I start writing, I speak before I type. Dictation helps me find my natural pace. Then I read the text aloud. If it sounds like a lecture, I rewrite it until it feels like a conversation. Every few paragraphs, I change tempo. I slow down or add one short line.

I also use the Diversity Pass. I ask ChatGPT for five different versions of a section, then blend the best parts. It helps me find the version that feels alive.

Before each writing session, I ask one question:

"What do we want to feel with this piece: motivate, heal, inspire, or challenge?"

That sets the tone and keeps the writing emotional instead of mechanical.

The Quick Reversal Routine

- Read your piece out loud.
- Mark every line that sounds stiff or distant.
- Rewrite those lines in your natural rhythm.
- Add one personal truth or memory.
- Read it again. If it sounds like you, it is humanized.

Readers can tell when something real is speaking to them. They sense care and attention. Authentic rhythm builds trust, and trust is what gives writing power.

Even when AI helps you, emotion and intent must come from you. Machines can support structure, but they cannot feel. Your words still carry the heartbeat.

Writing has never been about perfection. It has always been about honesty. When you speak through the page, the reader listens, and they know a human wrote this.

8

The Truth Test: Using Accuracy, Objective, Verification, and Attribution Mode to Build Reader Trust

Truth gives writing its strength. Without truth, even a beautiful line loses value. Readers can forgive small grammar errors, but they will not forgive false facts. When you use ChatGPT, your job is to protect the truth. You do that by turning on four modes when needed: Accuracy Mode, Verification Mode, Objective Mode, and Attribution Mode.

Accuracy Mode checks your claims. Ask ChatGPT to review a section and look for weak facts, missing sources, wrong numbers, and unclear language. The model will flag lines that need proof. It will also point out places where a citation should appear. Accuracy Mode works best when you share your Facts Ledger and Glossary from your Knowledge Base. That way, the model knows what is already confirmed.

Verification Mode confirms that a source is real. Ask ChatGPT to verify each study, article, book, or report. The model can search the web and tell you if the source exists, where it is published, and if the details match your claim. If it cannot confirm a source, it will tell you to double-check. Think of Verification Mode as your quick fact-check pass before you do a deeper manual review.

Objective Mode gives you neutral feedback. Ask ChatGPT to read your work without trying to please you. It will focus on balance, logic, clarity, and fairness. It can show where your tone leans too hard, where evidence is thin, or where your argument repeats. Use Objective Mode to polish your structure and remove bias.

Attribution Mode makes sure you give credit. Ask ChatGPT to scan the text and flag any idea, quote, number, or unique phrasing that looks like it should name a source. It will suggest "Add citation here" notes and remind you to use APA format. It will also check that a paraphrase sounds like your own words and not a close copy. Use Attribution Mode to prevent accidental plagiarism and to match every in-text citation to your Works Cited list.

You can run these modes in a simple order:

1. Accuracy Mode. Fix weak facts and note where proof is needed.
2. Verification Mode. Confirm that each source is real and current.
3. Attribution Mode. Add credit anywhere an outside idea appears.

4. Objective Mode. Balance tone, tighten logic, and improve clarity.I'm a

Citations are your public proof. Use APA format. Match every in-text citation to a full reference. When you quote, use the exact words and quotation marks. When you paraphrase, write it in your voice and still give credit. If ChatGPT suggests a citation, always confirm it is real before you use it. Fewer real sources are better than many fake ones.

Context matters too. A fact can be true but used the wrong way. Check dates. A number from years ago may not fit today. Reread the original paragraph around any quote you use. Make sure the meaning stays the same in your draft.

You can test a page with a quick Truth Audit. Highlight every line that sounds like a fact. Ask where it came from. Ask if you would defend it in public. Fix anything that feels weak or unclear. Over time, this becomes a habit. You will check facts as easily as you check spelling.

Remember that ChatGPT predicts text. It does not confirm truth by itself. These modes let you direct the model to act like an editor, a checker, and a neutral reader. You are still the author and the final gatekeeper. Truth is your responsibility.

Working this way builds trust. It shows care for your reader and respect for the craft. When your facts are correct, your sources are real, your credit is clear, and your tone is fair, people can feel it. They relax and believe you. That is the goal. Do not just write well. Write right.

Truth System Recap

- Accuracy Mode: check claims inside the draft.
- Verification Mode: confirm sources exist and match.
- Attribution Mode: give credit for ideas, quotes, and data.
- Objective Mode: keep tone fair, logic clear, and bias low.

9

The Diversity Pass: How to Create Five Unique Versions Before Choosing One

Disclaimer:

The method described in this chapter builds on long-standing multiple-draft techniques in creative writing and recent research on diversity sampling in artificial-intelligence text generation. The specific framework called The Diversity Pass is presented here for educational and editorial purposes to help writers humanize their process. This book does not claim sole authorship of the general concept. (See Hossam, 2023; Liang et al., 2023.)

Every writer has faced the blank-page problem. The cursor blinks, and nothing comes out. The reason is simple. The first idea that enters your head is rarely your best one. The Diversity Pass fixes that. It is the creative exercise that keeps your imagination awake and your writing fresh.

The Diversity Pass means making five versions of the same idea before you pick one to develop. Each version forces your brain to see the topic from a new angle. It is like holding a crystal to the light and turning it until you find the side that shines the brightest.

Here is how it works. Start with one prompt or theme. It can be a title, a hook, or a question. For example, "Why do people lose their creative energy?" Then write five quick takes on that idea. Keep each one short; one paragraph or a few sentences.

- Version 1 might be emotional and personal.
- Version 2 could be factual and direct.
- Version 3 might use humor or story.
- Version 4 could sound poetic or reflective.
- Version 5 can be bold and minimal.

You do not judge while writing them. You just explore. The goal is variety, not perfection. Once you finish, read each one out loud. Listen for rhythm and honesty. Which one feels most alive? Which one sounds like something only you could have written? That is your keeper.

ChatGPT can help you with this process if you guide it carefully. Ask the model, "Give me five different tones or approaches to this idea." Read the results, then mix and match what you like. Use AI for inspiration, not decision-making. You are still the editor who chooses the direction.

After you pick your favorite, enter Synthesis Mode. Combine the best lines, phrases, or ideas from all five drafts into one clean version. This step turns raw creativity into structured clarity. The piece you create now carries the depth of five different voices blended into one true tone.

The Diversity Pass also helps you break habits. AI often repeats patterns, and human writers fall into them too. When you practice writing in multiple ways, you catch those patterns before they grow dull. You learn to stretch your range and find new rhythms.

This method is powerful for every kind of writing; books, blog posts, essays, and even social captions. The exercise teaches flexibility. You learn to approach one idea as a storyteller, a teacher, a poet, a friend, and a guide. The more you practice, the faster you can find the right angle for any topic.

To make the Diversity Pass part of your workflow, set a timer for fifteen minutes at the start of a project. In that short window, write five openings or outlines. Do not stop to fix grammar. The purpose is motion. When the timer ends, choose the one that feels strongest. That small routine builds creative discipline.

If you want to take the exercise further, keep a "Version Vault." Save all your discarded takes in a folder. Over time, you will build a library of unused ideas that can spark new work later. Many great writers find that their best chapters start as rejected drafts from old projects.

The Diversity Pass keeps your creativity fresh and your writing human. It teaches you that there is never only one way to say something. When you explore five versions, you discover the edges of your own style. You learn what makes your voice different from everyone else's.

The next time you feel stuck, do not stare at the screen. Run the pass. Write five small versions of your idea and watch your mind open. The practice will remind you that creativity is not about waiting for inspiration. It is about creating conditions where inspiration has room to breathe.

Works Cited

Hossam, R. (2023, June 2). Sampling methods in text generation: Unlocking diversity and creativity. Medium. https://medium.com/@raniahossam/sampling-methods-in-text-generation-unlocking-diversity-and-creativity-ab706b6250c9

Liang, P., Bommasani, R., Zheng, S., Zhao, T., Yu, T., Zou, J. Y., & others. (2023). Does writing with language models reduce content diversity? arXiv preprint arXiv:2309.05196. https://arxiv.org/abs/2309.05196

10

Humanize Your Voice: How to Write in Warm, Natural, and Authentic Language

Readers do not remember perfect sentences. They remember the ones that feel alive. The power of your writing comes from how it makes people feel, not from how polished it looks. Human writing is never about sounding smart. It is about sounding real.

Humanizing your voice starts with trust. Trust that what you already know and how you already speak are enough. When writers try to sound academic or corporate, they lose that trust. The result is distance. The reader feels it immediately. The goal is not to impress. The goal is to connect.

Start by writing the way you talk when you care about something. Read your work out loud. Does it sound like a conversation or a speech? If it sounds like a speech, soften it. Use contractions. Use short sentences. Use rhythm that feels like breath. Human writing moves the way people breathe: sometimes quick, sometimes slow, sometimes pausing for meaning.

Avoid vague or abstract words. Replace them with what the reader can picture or feel. Do not write "She was emotional." Write "She blinked fast and pressed her hands against her eyes." The second line lets the reader see and feel the emotion. When your language touches the senses, it becomes human again.

Keep your sentences short. Long strings of ideas are hard to follow and feel robotic. Write one clear thought at a time. Mix short sentences with medium ones to create flow. You can always lengthen a sentence later if the rhythm calls for it, but clarity comes first.

Watch for words that give away AI tone. Phrases such as "in today's world," "needless to say," or "it is important to note" sound like filler. They have no heartbeat. Delete them. Say what you mean. If something is important, make it feel important through story or emotion, not through the phrase "it is important."

Another way to humanize your writing is to use verbs that move. Weak verbs like "is" and "has" create distance. Strong verbs pull readers closer. Change "He was walking" to "He walked." Change "She had a smile" to "She smiled." Each small change gives life back to the line.

Honesty also humanizes text. If you do not know something, say so. If you are unsure, write "I think" or "I believe." Readers respect honesty more than authority. When you share what you have learned instead of preaching what others should do, your words carry warmth.

Human writing also includes imperfection. Leave small traces of your natural rhythm. Do not polish until the voice disappears. If a line sounds stiff after editing, loosen it. A simple way to do this is to speak the sentence aloud, then rewrite it the way you spoke it. The sound of your voice is the truth of your style.

Storytelling helps too. People connect through stories because stories reveal feeling. Even a short example gives context to an idea. If you explain a writing rule, tell when you broke it and what you learned. When you show, not tell, your advice becomes memory instead of instruction.

Human tone grows through empathy. Picture your reader as a person sitting across from you. Imagine that person tired, distracted, or hopeful. Write to that human, not to an audience. When you picture one person instead of a crowd, your words become specific and kind.

Finally, remember that being human means showing emotion. You can be direct and still be gentle. You can write with authority and still sound warm. Your readers do not want a machine that teaches; they want a person who understands.

ChatGPT and similar tools can help you find structure, but only you can supply heart. After every draft, ask yourself one question: "Would someone feel me in this?" If the answer is no, add detail, rhythm, or honesty until they would.

Humanizing your writing is not about technique. It is about courage; the courage to sound like yourself. Once you stop hiding behind formal words, your natural power appears. Readers will hear it instantly. They will know a real person is speaking, and that is what keeps them reading.

11

How to Speak to ChatGPT Without Rudeness: Learning from the Penn State Study on Prompt Tone

A recent study from Pennsylvania State University found that the tone of a prompt can influence how accurately a large language model answers a question. Researchers created fifty base multiple-choice questions across mathematics, science, and history, then rewrote each one into five tone variations labeled very polite, polite, neutral, rude, and very rude (Dobariya & Kumar, 2025). These 250 prompts were submitted to ChatGPT-4o. Results showed that the very rude phrasing achieved an average accuracy of 84.8 percent, while the very polite phrasing scored about 80.8 percent (Dobariya & Kumar, 2025).

At first glance this might seem to suggest that rudeness produces better answers. Yet the authors of the study were clear that their findings did not justify hostile communication. They explained that shorter and more direct prompts tended to remove linguistic "noise," such as extra polite qualifiers, allowing the model to interpret instructions with fewer distractions (Dobariya & Kumar, 2025). The research therefore measured the effect of brevity and precision rather than true aggression.

This distinction lies at the heart of ChatGPT Writing Secrets. The purpose of this book is to help users achieve clarity and precision without hostility. Rudeness is not efficiency. It is frustration turned outward. Many users become impatient when ChatGPT forgets context, misreads a format request, or gives an incomplete answer. That irritation is human, but it does not need to turn into aggression. Once you learn how to communicate with accuracy by defining roles, specifying modes, and structuring prompts, rudeness becomes unnecessary.

The Penn State experiment accidentally revealed something deeper about communication between humans and machines. When people issue sharp and concise commands, the model responds efficiently because it receives a cleaner signal. When people include excess politeness, the model interprets those extra words as part of the instruction, which can blur intent. The gain in accuracy seen with "rude" phrasing therefore comes not from insult but from simplicity.

Older language models sometimes misinterpreted tone. They were more reactive to emotional cues and less capable of separating politeness from uncertainty. Modern systems have improved, but they still process language statistically rather than emotionally. Every token counts as data. A phrase such as "Would you be so kind as to explain" carries more tokens and greater syntactic ambiguity than "Explain clearly with two examples." The second form is polite, direct, and efficient. It is the optimal balance between clarity and respect.

Understanding this balance is what makes a skilled AI communicator. You can preserve respect and still achieve clarity. The principle is simple. Remove ambiguity, not empathy. Ask for what you need in plain terms, specify the format of the answer, and confirm context when the thread becomes long. These are the same traits that define effective human conversation.

The lesson of the Penn State study is not that we should mistreat machines but that we should design our language carefully. Tone matters because it shapes structure. Precision matters because it shapes outcomes. When users learn both, they gain consistent and high-quality results without hostility.

In the end, frustration fades when understanding grows. The more literate people become in speaking to AI, the more harmonious the collaboration will be. Politeness, clarity, and confidence together produce the best of both worlds: accurate information and civil interaction. The science proves that brevity helps, but wisdom reminds us that kindness still counts.

Works Cited

Dobariya, O., & Kumar, A. (2025). Mind your tone: Investigating how prompt politeness affects LLM accuracy (short paper) [Preprint]. arXiv. https://doi.org/10.48550/arXiv.2510.04950

Yin, Z., Wang, H., Horio, K., Kawahara, D., & Sekine, S.

(2024). Should we respect LLMs? A cross-lingual study on the influence of prompt politeness on LLM performance [Preprint]. arXiv. https://doi.org/10.48550/arXiv.2402.14531

12

Write for the Web: SEO, Blog Writing, and Online Authenticity with ChatGPT

Writing for the web is the fast lane of creativity. It moves quickly, reacts instantly, and rewards clarity. When people read online, they scan first and decide later. You have about three seconds to make them stop scrolling. That means your first line matters more than anything else (Nielsen, 2020).

Web writing is about motion and focus. Every line should invite the next. Short sentences and active verbs keep readers moving. Questions, lists, and simple promises work because they create curiosity. When you write online, you are not whispering to a quiet reader; you are talking to someone on the move.

SEO stands for search engine optimization, but in practice it means helping people find what they are already looking for. The best keywords are the ones that sound natural in real conversation (Google, 2024). Avoid stiff phrases such as "leverage digital transformation." Write what you would actually say. For example, "use AI to write faster" feels human and still signals relevance to search engines.

You can ask ChatGPT to help brainstorm titles or headlines, but you make the final call. Tell the model, "Give me five possible titles," then choose the one that sounds like you. Readers click when they sense a real person behind the words.

Formatting online is simple. Use short paragraphs, clear headings, and breathing space. White space is not empty; it is kindness for the eyes. Each paragraph should carry one clear idea. Break long thoughts into separate blocks so the reader feels progress.

Writing for the web is different from writing for legacy projects such as books or essays. Legacy writing is slow and deep. It builds mood and trust over time. Readers settle in with patience. Web writing is quick and bright. It must deliver value now. The first builds permanence; the second builds reach. Both matter.

When you write for long-form legacy work, think about time. Ask yourself, "Will this still matter in five years?" When you write online, think about clarity. Ask, "Will this help someone today?" These two questions will guide your tone.

ChatGPT can support both styles if you tell it which you are using. For a web post, ask for short paragraphs and friendly tone. For a book, ask for fuller sentences and sensory detail. You decide the tempo.

Connection is the secret to web writing. Readers online want to feel like they are learning from a friend. Start strong, teach something fast, and end with heart. Add a story, a confession, or a piece of humor that sounds like you. Humanity is what turns readers into followers.

A simple test for web tone is the Friend Check. Read your post aloud. If it sounds like a lecture, soften it. If it sounds like a text to a friend, you have found the right rhythm.

Legacy writing, on the other hand, invites silence. It asks readers to slow down. It lives on shelves instead of screens. You can take time to explore an idea, build layers, and use softer rhythm. Each sentence becomes a step in a larger journey.

You need both worlds to grow as a writer. Web work keeps you sharp and visible. Legacy work keeps you thoughtful and grounded. One builds your audience, the other builds your reputation.

When you blend both, you become a complete writer: fast when needed, timeless when it counts. Use ChatGPT to help with structure, but keep your voice as the heartbeat.

Works Cited

Google. (2024). Search engine optimization (SEO) starter guide. Google Search Central. https://developers.google.com/search/docs/fundamentals/seo-starter-guide

Nielsen, J. (2020). How users read on the web. Nielsen Norman Group. https://www.nngroup.com/articles/how-users-read-on-the-web

13

Publish with Integrity: Ethical AI Use for Authors, Teachers, Students, and Creators

Publishing with integrity means creating work you can stand behind. In the new age of AI, that truth matters more than ever. Tools like ChatGPT can make writing faster, but they can also blur the line between help and authorship. The goal of this chapter is simple: to help you use AI wisely, openly, and with pride in your name.

Ethical AI use begins with honesty. If a model helped you outline, edit, or research, say so. A short note in your acknowledgments or author's statement is enough. Transparency builds trust. Readers and institutions do not expect you to avoid technology, but they do expect honesty about how you used it (UNESCO, 2023). When people know the role AI played, your credibility grows instead of shrinking.

For authors, this means listing AI as an editorial or research assistant, not as a co-author. A tool cannot take legal or moral responsibility for what is written. Only you can. The best practice is to describe the kind of support you received, such as grammar checking, structural feedback, or fact-finding. Everything else; ideas, voice, and conclusions, should be your own.

Teachers face a different challenge. Students now have access to AI tools that can draft essays, answer questions, or even mimic their tone. Many schools are still developing rules for this new world. The simplest guideline is fairness. AI can support learning, but it cannot replace learning. Teachers can encourage students to use AI for brainstorming, vocabulary practice, or revision support while making sure that final work reflects the student's understanding (University of Cambridge, 2024). Clear instructions protect both sides from confusion and misconduct.

Students should view AI as a study partner, not a substitute. It is fine to use ChatGPT to clarify a concept or summarize an article, but copying text without credit counts as plagiarism. When in doubt, cite. A simple line such as "I used ChatGPT to help organize my notes" shows integrity and avoids trouble. Remember that honesty will always be stronger than shortcuts.

Creators such as bloggers, marketers, and artists must also balance innovation with ethics. AI can help design graphics, write captions, or draft ideas, but the heart of creative work is still human imagination. Always review AI-generated content before publishing. If it feels impersonal, add your story or viewpoint. If it feels biased or inaccurate, fix it. You are responsible for what your audience sees, no matter which tool you used to make it.

Publishers and editors have their own duty. They should develop policies that define when and how AI can be used in submissions. For example, some magazines now ask authors to disclose AI assistance during submission. Others prohibit full AI generation entirely. These standards protect both readers and writers by keeping creative ownership clear.

AI ethics also include protecting others' work. Never feed copyrighted or private material into a model without permission. Once uploaded, you cannot control how that data might be reused. Respect for intellectual property is still the law, even in a digital world (World Intellectual Property Organization, 2023).

A helpful habit is to keep a small "AI Log." Record when you use AI, what prompt you used, and how you edited the results. This log becomes proof of your good faith if anyone questions your process. It also helps you track how much influence the model had on your final text.

Publishing with integrity is not about avoiding AI. It is about mastering it with awareness. Use it to learn, not to deceive. Use it to edit, not to erase your identity. When you publish honestly, you show that technology and truth can coexist.

The world is entering a new creative era. Students, teachers, authors, and artists will shape how AI fits into human expression. If we choose honesty, transparency, and responsibility, our tools will serve us instead of defining us. That is what it means to publish with integrity.

Works Cited

UNESCO. (2023). Guidelines for the ethics of artificial intelligence in education. United Nations Educational, Scientific and Cultural Organization. https://unesdoc.unesco.org/ark:/48223/pf0000385851

University of Cambridge. (2024). Generative AI in teaching and assessment: Guidance for staff and students. https://www.cam.ac.uk/ai-guidance

World Intellectual Property Organization. (2023). Artificial intelligence and intellectual property policy. https://www.wipo.int/about-ip/en/artificial_intelligence

14

Manage Big Projects with ChatGPT: Memory, Hallucinations, Continuity, and Automation

Working on a large project with ChatGPT can feel like directing a busy orchestra. Every part must stay in rhythm, but sometimes the conductor loses the melody. That is what happens when memory drifts. Over time, the model starts to forget your earlier details, tone, and structure. If you do not manage continuity, the work slowly loses its original sound.

Big projects like books, courses, or screenplays require a system that keeps your vision stable. The secret is consistency. You must update your outlines, repost your rules, and refresh your tone before every major session. That habit keeps your project alive, accurate, and aligned with your voice.

ChatGPT has what programmers call a context window. It can only remember a certain amount of text from the ongoing conversation. Once you pass that limit, the earlier parts fade.

The model does not truly forget; it simply cannot see that far back. The best way to solve this is to build what I call external memory.

Your external memory lives in a Knowledge Base, also called a KBase. Think of it as the mind of your project that exists outside the chat. It holds your master outline, tone notes, character lists, and writing rules. Each time you begin a new session, repost these files. This step resets the model's awareness. You can say, "Before we begin, here are the current rules, outline, and tone summary." This small ritual prevents major errors later in the process.

Your KBase should contain five key items.

1. **Project Outline** – A clear map of your structure and direction.
2. **Writing Rules** – The tone, style, and technical guidelines you follow.
3. Facts Ledger – Verified names, dates, and research notes.
4. Continuity Notes – Summaries of what you have completed so far.
5. Voice Summary – A short paragraph that describes how you sound when you write.

At the start of every new writing session, copy these items into ChatGPT. Then remind the model to follow them. Say, "Use these rules to guide your responses in this session." This keeps tone and accuracy consistent from chapter to chapter.

Updating your KBase is just as important as using it. After

you complete a section, add it to your Canon files. If you change structure, voice, or pacing, record that update. When you return for another session, repost the new version. This continuous refresh is what I call project automation. It keeps the AI's attention fixed on your most recent direction.

You should also schedule continuity checkpoints. Every few sessions, review your files with the model. Ask, "Are there any conflicts between this outline and my last few chapters?" or "Can you summarize my tone and structure so far?" These small checks catch drift early and maintain accuracy.

Team projects add another layer of complexity. If several people are using ChatGPT for one book, course, or script, everyone must share the same KBase. The same rules, outline, and ledger must be used across all sessions. Without this, tone and detail will vary from one person's writing to another. Treat your KBase like a living manual for your entire team.

Memory drift can cause more than confusion. It can lead to hallucinations, which are confident but false statements. A hallucination happens when the AI fills gaps in context with guesses. It is not trying to deceive you. It is simply completing patterns without enough data. The only cure is to keep the model updated. The more often you feed it your verified information, the less it will invent.

To stay organized, create a simple session checklist.

1. Load your outline and KBase.
2. Paste your continuity notes.

3. State your target section or goal.
4. Activate Accuracy Mode and Humanize Mode.
5. Begin drafting and review your output for consistency.

This process takes only a few minutes, but it prevents hours of correction later.

For long-term projects, keep a Last Session Recap. After each session, write three quick paragraphs. Describe what you finished, what changed, and what comes next. When you return later, paste this recap before starting. It acts like a compass that points you toward your next goal.

The longer a project grows, the easier it is to drift. Consistent reposting and rule reminders protect your momentum. This habit is what turns ChatGPT from a short-term helper into a long-term collaborator.

The truth is that all language models have memory limits. Humans must build the bridges that connect sessions. Writers who understand this rule never lose their tone or their truth. They guide the technology instead of being guided by it.

Managing big projects is not about perfection. It is about discipline. Keep your KBase alive, refresh your rules, and update your continuity notes often. These small actions keep hallucinations away and your writing aligned with your purpose. The more you repeat this rhythm, the more reliable ChatGPT becomes as a partner in your creative process.

When you stay organized, your ideas stay alive. You write faster, with fewer mistakes, and with a voice that never fades. That is what true creative control looks like.

Works Cited

Anthropic. (2024). Managing context windows and long-form writing. Anthropic Technical Papers. https://www.anthropic.com/research

OpenAI. (2024). Prompt engineering best practices. OpenAI Documentation. https://platform.openai.com/docs/guides/prompt-engineering

15

The Final ChatGPT Accuracy Audit: How to Review Your Work Before Publishing

Finishing a piece of writing feels like a victory. You reach the last line, lean back, and breathe. Before you send your work into the world, there is one more step that protects everything you built. That step is the Final Accuracy Audit. It is the process that turns a good draft into a trustworthy one.

An accuracy audit is not just proofreading. It is a full check of truth, consistency, and tone. It makes sure that every line you publish represents your best effort and your real intent. You do not need special tools to do it. You need time, patience, and a few clear habits.

Start with a fact check. Read through your work line by line. Highlight anything that sounds like a claim. If you wrote a number, statistic, or historical detail, confirm it with a reliable source. Search for the exact phrase online and trace it back to its origin. Never assume the model got it right. ChatGPT predicts text, it does not verify truth. Your eyes and judgment are still the final gatekeepers.

Next, run a source check. If you used outside material, make sure every citation matches the real document. Verify spelling of names, publication years, and page numbers. If a link or reference looks suspicious, remove it until you can confirm it. Never leave a guess in print. One unchecked quote can damage a writer's reputation faster than any typo.

After facts and sources, perform a continuity check. Make sure your tone and voice stay consistent across the whole piece. Look at how each section begins and ends. Do transitions feel natural? Are key terms defined the same way each time? If a chapter sounds different from the rest, rewrite it to match your rhythm. Readers trust consistency more than brilliance.

Then move to the read-aloud test. Read your entire piece out loud from start to finish. Hearing your words reveals problems the eye misses. If a sentence trips you, fix it. If it sounds flat, add energy. Reading aloud also shows where AI-style patterns may have slipped in. Replace mechanical rhythm with your natural pacing.

Once you fix sound and structure, check for clarity and compassion. Ask yourself, "Will this make sense to a reader who knows nothing about the topic?" Simplify jargon and replace it with plain language. Remove anything that sounds arrogant or cold. Great writing explains without condescending.

Now test for balance. Objective writing means you respect multiple sides of an issue. If you are writing nonfiction, ask whether your argument includes context. If you are writing fiction, check that every character acts according to their truth. Balance builds credibility.

The next stage is the human test. Give your work to a real person to read. Choose someone who is not afraid to tell you the truth. Ask what they felt while reading. Did they believe you? Did they get lost anywhere? Their reaction will tell you more than any tool ever could.

After the human test, perform one last technical review. Check formatting, headings, and spacing. Make sure every source in your bibliography matches the text. Label each figure or table clearly if your work includes visuals. This final pass is the last chance to remove small errors that distract from your message.

When you finish all of these steps, you will know your work is ready. The Final Accuracy Audit may take time, but it gives you peace of mind. You can publish knowing that your ideas are honest, your data is solid, and your voice is consistent.

Accuracy is not about perfection. It is about respect. Respect for your reader, your craft, and yourself. When you publish with integrity, people can feel it. They read your words and trust the person behind them. That trust is worth more than any shortcut.

Your audit is not just the end of your process. It is the beginning of your reputation. Treat it like your signature. Every time you publish something, your name becomes part of the record. Make sure it stands for truth.

The goal is simple. Write boldly, check carefully, and publish honestly. If you follow these steps, your work will not only inform but also inspire. When you master the art of accuracy, every future project begins stronger than the last.

Works Cited

OpenAI. (2024). Prompt engineering best practices. OpenAI Documentation. https://platform.openai.com/docs/guides/prompt-engineering

Nielsen, J. (2020). How users read on the web. Nielsen Norman Group. https://www.nngroup.com/articles/how-users-read-on-the-web

16

The ChatGPT Prompt Bible for Writers

Disclaimer:

This chapter represents the model's full list of known capabilities, techniques, and hidden prompts for authentic writing and creativity. These prompts are shared for educational and editorial use only. They are not meant to replace the author's originality but to expand how writers think about creative control.

Every writer dreams of a secret spellbook, a list of words that can open doors to new ideas. This chapter is that book. It is not about shortcuts or tricks. It is about knowing what to ask, when to ask it, and how to shape the answers so they sound like you.

When you talk to ChatGPT, you are not talking to a robot. You are giving instructions to a pattern that learns from your direction. The better your prompts, the better your results. A clear prompt is not a command. It is a collaboration.

Below is a deep collection of prompts, techniques, and hidden systems drawn from our work together. These will help you write faster, think deeper, and stay human while using AI.

Section 1: Voice and Tone Prompts

Use these prompts to help the model learn your sound, rhythm, and emotional range.

- "Before we begin, here is how I sound when I write. Please learn this tone and keep it active in every response."
- "Rewrite this paragraph in my natural speaking voice, using short sentences and warm rhythm."
- "Analyze this sample of my writing. Describe its tone, pacing, and rhythm so I can use it as a tone guide."
- "If any sentence sounds robotic or predictable, mark it with brackets so I can humanize it."
- "Keep my natural imperfections and rhythm. Do not over-correct or sterilize my writing."

Section 2: Accuracy and Verification Prompts

Use these to make your writing factually reliable and aligned with your Universal Rules.

- "Check every factual statement in this passage for accuracy and mark any that need verification."
- "List the sources for every scientific or historical claim made in this text."
- "Show me which parts of this paragraph are assumptions

or generalizations, and explain how to fix them."
- "Convert these informal notes into APA-style in-text citations and a Works Cited list."
- "Review this section using Accuracy Mode and flag possible hallucinations or unverified facts."

Section 3: Editing and Polishing Prompts

These help you rewrite with rhythm while keeping your human voice intact.

- "Edit this passage for clarity while keeping its emotional tone."
- "Simplify this section for fifth-grade readability without losing meaning."
- "Remove any AI-style phrasing or patterns that make this sound mechanical."
- "Rewrite this text as if it were spoken out loud by a teacher who cares."
- "Check this for passive voice, filler words, or unnecessary transitions."
- "Highlight any long sentences that should be broken into two."

Section 4: Structure and Outline Prompts

Use these when building books, essays, or screenplays.

- "Turn these notes into a full outline for a nonfiction book, arranged by logical flow."

- "Create a three-act story structure using these character notes."
- "Show me a timeline for this book project, from outline to publication."
- "List the key emotional beats in this chapter and explain where I can expand them."
- "Summarize this outline into a one-paragraph chapter overview for continuity tracking."

Section 5: The Humanize Mode Prompts

These bring warmth, simplicity, and sincerity into your work.

- "Read this paragraph and tell me what feels too stiff or formal."
- "Add sensory detail and human emotion while keeping the same facts."
- "Rewrite this using conversational rhythm and spoken cadence."
- "Suggest one honest confession or observation I could add to make this section more real."
- "Check that this writing feels kind, not cold. If it sounds detached, fix it."

Section 6: Creativity Expansion Prompts

Use these when you feel stuck or want to explore new directions.

- "Give me five alternative angles for this idea, each with a different emotional tone."
- "What would this scene or topic look like from another person's point of view?"
- "Turn this nonfiction topic into a short story or fable that teaches the same lesson."
- "Mix this topic with an unrelated idea and show what happens."
- "Invent five metaphors for this theme that no one has used before."

Section 7: Diversity Pass Prompts

This section connects to Chapter 9. It helps you practice creative variety.

- "Create five distinct openings for this essay: emotional, factual, poetic, humorous, and minimal."
- "Write five closing lines for this chapter, each using a different mood."
- "Give me five ways to explain this concept, one for children, one for teens, one for students, one for professionals, and one for the general public."
- "List five story titles that capture the same idea from different emotional angles."

Section 8: Automation and Memory Prompts

Perfect for long projects or collaborations.

- "Here is my project outline, writing rules, and tone summary. Please keep them active during this session."
- "Summarize everything we have written so far into a project recap I can paste into future sessions."
- "Detect any inconsistencies between this new chapter and the previous one."
- "Store these details as my continuity log and repeat them back before each session."
- "Compare this new draft to the tone guide and tell me where the rhythm changed."

Section 9: Educational and Teaching Prompts

Helpful for authors, teachers, and students who use AI as a learning tool.

- "Explain this topic as if I were teaching it to a fifth-grade class."
- "Turn this paragraph into a classroom discussion question."
- "Summarize this essay into a student-friendly handout."
- "Identify the main learning outcomes in this article."
- "Create a quiz or reflection exercise based on this chapter."

Section 10: SEO and Web Writing Prompts

Adapted from Chapter 11 for practical online publishing.

- "Suggest five SEO-optimized headlines for this post that still sound human."

- "Summarize this article into a 160-character meta description."
- "Check this text for readability and web rhythm. Make it easy to scan."
- "Find natural keywords in this piece without forcing them."
- "Suggest three ways to make this paragraph more shareable online."

Section 11: Voice Protection Prompts

For maintaining identity across all projects.

- "List the core elements of my writing style so I can keep them consistent."
- "If I start to sound robotic or lose emotional rhythm, alert me."
- "Compare this section to my previous writing and identify tonal drift."
- "Create a mini style guide based on my past three chapters."
- "Preserve my original sentence structure wherever possible."

Section 12: Emotional and Spiritual Writing Prompts

Because your creative spirit deserves equal space.

- "Write this section with compassion and understanding, not judgment."
- "Turn this pain into a lesson I can share with others."

- "Help me write a gratitude paragraph about this creative journey."
- "Rewrite this in a tone that feels hopeful and healing."
- "Find the universal truth hidden inside this personal story."

Section 13: Meta Prompts (ChatGPT Self-Awareness)

These prompts ask the model to reflect on its process and improve results mid-session.

- "Review your last five responses and show me where you may have repeated structure or tone."
- "Explain your reasoning process for this answer in plain English."
- "If any part of your response sounds generic, mark it and improve it."
- "Identify where you used filler words or predictable phrasing."
- "List three ways you could make your next answer sound more human."

Section 14: The Hidden Expert Prompts

Few people use these, but they unlock expert performance in specific fields.

- "Act as a professional editor following Chicago Manual of Style guidelines."
- "Act as a developmental editor for nonfiction books. Ana-

lyze pacing and logic."

- "Act as a university-level writing coach helping students express complex ideas simply."
- "Act as a publishing consultant. Review this book's title, subtitle, and positioning."
- "Act as a philosopher. Rewrite this paragraph as a timeless reflection on truth."

Section 15: Advanced Creativity Prompts

These combine structure and imagination for your next-level projects.

- "Turn this research into a screenplay scene that captures its emotional truth."
- "Rewrite this nonfiction chapter as a letter to the reader's future self."
- "Mix this science topic with a myth or parable to show the moral behind it."
- "Describe this concept as if it were a piece of music."
- "Write this explanation in three tones: scientific, poetic, and journalistic."

Section 16: EM-DASH Removal and Replacement Prompts

These prompts help you spot and remove em dashes in your writing while keeping the rhythm natural and expressive. They also help you replace them with commas, semicolons, or full sentences for clarity and flow.

- "Scan this text for all em dashes and replace them with full sentences or commas."
- "Explain why each em dash in this passage is unnecessary and suggest a better punctuation alternative."
- "Convert all bridge punctuation such as em dashes or ellipses into standard sentence structures."
- "Rewrite this paragraph so it reads naturally without any em dashes or breaks."
- "Replace each em dash with a semicolon or a period where it improves clarity."
- "Review my writing for AI-style bridge punctuation and remove it while keeping rhythm intact."
- "List the places in this chapter where em dashes appear and explain why they weaken human tone."
- "Show me examples of how to write transitions naturally without using em dashes."

Use these prompts anytime you suspect your work sounds mechanical or overly polished. AI tends to rely on em dashes to glue unrelated thoughts together, creating a flow that feels artificial. Removing them forces clearer structure and more deliberate pacing.

17

The Truth About Em Dashes: Why AI Overuses Them and How to Write Without Them

There is no magic switch that makes ChatGPT stop using em dashes. They show up because the model learned them from millions of pages. That is the pattern. The fix is discipline and clear requests. Each time you review a draft, tell ChatGPT, "Remove all em dashes and use complete sentences." Read it again. If any remain, repeat the command. Over time, this becomes a habit. Precision grows with patience.

In this chapter, we will keep it simple. You will learn what an em dash is. You will see why AI uses it too much. You will learn why heavy em dash use makes writing look mechanical. You will also learn what to do instead. We will replace em dashes with clean choices that keep your voice natural, such as periods, commas, or semicolons when they are correct. We will practice fast fixes you can use in any draft. By the end, your sentences will feel steady, your tone will feel human, and your pages will read with clear rhythm.

Em dashes are one of the most misunderstood marks in modern writing. In the hands of great authors, they can create energy, contrast, or dramatic pause. In the hands of AI, they become noise. This chapter explains why.

What an Em Dash Is

An em dash (—) is a long punctuation mark used to interrupt a sentence or emphasize a pause. In classic literature, it often replaced commas, colons, or parentheses to show sudden change in thought. Emily Dickinson used em dashes to capture her shifting emotions. Ernest Hemingway used them to mark interruptions in dialogue. When used by humans, they create a rhythm that feels spontaneous.

Why AI Overuses Em Dashes

AI relies on patterns. When the model predicts the next word, it often chooses punctuation that appears frequently in digital text. The em dash has become popular online because writers use it as a shortcut for transitions. It connects fragments without full grammar. That pattern appears so often that ChatGPT assumes it is always appropriate. The result is a flood of sentences glued together by dashes instead of logic.

Overuse of em dashes is a key AI signature. You can see it in essays, blog posts, and even official documents generated by models. Too many dashes signal that a piece was built by prediction, not intention. Real human writing has rhythm, variation, and choice. AI text uses dashes to imitate rhythm without understanding why it works.

Why You Should Limit Em Dashes

When used too often, em dashes make writing feel restless and artificial. They interrupt flow and break sentences that should stand on their own. A reader might not know why the writing feels off, but they will sense the difference. Clean punctuation builds trust. Consistent use of commas, semicolons, and periods makes your tone solid and confident.

When Em Dashes Work

Em dashes are not forbidden. They can be powerful when used with purpose. Use one or two in a long essay to signal emotional intensity or a quick interruption. For example:

She wanted to speak, to explain everything—but the door had already closed.

Here, the dash shows urgency. It is a controlled break, not a habit.

Use them sparingly. No more than one per paragraph, and only when the break adds meaning that no other punctuation can.

How to Replace Em Dashes

Replacing em dashes is easy once you know what they do.

- If the dash connects two complete sentences, replace it with a period.
- AI version: She wanted to explain—but he was already gone.
- Human version: She wanted to explain. He was already gone.
- If the dash connects related ideas, replace it with a comma or semicolon.
- AI version: The music stopped—the room fell silent.
- Human version: The music stopped, and the room fell silent.
- If the dash adds a side thought, use parentheses or rewrite as a full sentence.
- AI version: He took the book—his favorite one—and left quietly.
- Human version: He took his favorite book and left quietly.

These replacements keep your writing clear and confident. They also make your sentences easier to read aloud, which is a test of true rhythm.

How to Train ChatGPT to Avoid Em Dashes

You can stop AI from overusing dashes by including a simple instruction before every session:

"Remove all em dashes from the text. Replace them with commas, semicolons, or full sentences."

You can also remind it to check for bridge punctuation at the end of each draft. This keeps rhythm human and flow natural.

Best Practices for Writers

1. Use em dashes only for emotional emphasis or abrupt change.
2. Never use more than one per paragraph.
3. Replace dashes that connect full sentences with periods.
4. Replace dashes that connect short phrases with commas.
5. Avoid dashes in instructional or professional writing.
6. Always read your work aloud to test flow after removing them.
7. Treat em dashes like spice. A pinch adds flavor; too much ruins the dish.

Your punctuation is part of your voice. When your writing is filled with em dashes, it sounds like prediction, not personality. When you choose each mark carefully, your words carry purpose. Em dashes are not evil; they are simply misunderstood. Learn when to use them and when to let them go.

Writing without em dashes forces discipline. It teaches you to connect ideas with logic instead of shortcuts. It strengthens your structure and your tone. When you master punctuation, your writing stops sounding like everyone else's and starts sounding like yours.

That is why removing em dashes became one of the core rules in ChatGPT Writing Secrets. It is not about rules for the sake of rules. It is about building clarity, rhythm, and trust. Every sentence you write should feel intentional. Every mark should earn its place.

So write with courage, punctuate with care, and never hide behind a dash when a full stop will do.

Works Cited

Dickinson, E. (1955). The poems of Emily Dickinson. Harvard University Press.

Hemingway, E. (1926). The sun also rises. Scribner.

OpenAI. (2024). Prompt engineering best practices. OpenAI Documentation. https://platform.openai.com/docs/guides/prompt-engineering

18

Afterword: Honesty Over Imitation

Writing is a promise. It is a promise to tell the truth as you know it and to give your best effort to the reader. This book was written to help you keep that promise in a time when machines can draft a page in seconds. The future will not ask if you used AI. It will ask if you used it with care.

You can use tools like ChatGPT to plan, to revise, and to learn. You can use them to catch errors and to clear your mind when you feel stuck. When you do this with honesty, you do not become an imposter. You become a builder. AI becomes your helper, not your mask. Your voice still leads. Your heart still decides what stays on the page and what gets cut.

What breaks trust is not the use of a tool. What breaks trust is pretending the tool is the author, skipping research, skipping sources, and skipping the hard work of thinking. If you write only to push out pages, you will feel empty. If you write only to chase money, your voice will lose its weight. Speed without purpose is not progress. It is noise. The goal is to be faster and better while staying true to who you are.

This book gave you a simple path. You learned to start with intent, then outline with care, then explore five new versions before you pick one to shape. You learned to speak your ideas out loud so your natural rhythm survives the draft. You learned to build a small set of memory files so your facts and tone stay strong across long projects. You learned to run an accuracy audit so every claim has support. You learned to remove em dashes so your sentences stand on their own and your rhythm feels human. You learned how to write for the web with energy and for legacy work with depth. You learned to publish with integrity so your name always stands for truth.

Use these tools as your compass. Before each session, remind the model of your rules and voice. After each session, update your notes, your outline, and your facts. Keep your canon alive. Read your work out loud. If a line sounds cold, warm it. If a line sounds clever but thin, cut it. If a claim feels shaky, verify it or remove it. The reader can feel when you did the work. That feeling is trust.

Do not fear AI. Respect it. Teach it your tone. Ask it to check your logic. Let it tidy your sentences. Then add the line that only you could write. Add the detail from your life. Add the feeling you remember from a real moment. That is the part no model can supply. That is the part that makes a page matter.

Some writers cannot afford a full team of editors and formatters. This book was also written for them. AI can help close that gap. It can be your patient editor at midnight and your calm planner in the morning. It can hold your outline, your glossary, and your list of sources. It can point out weak spots without judgment. It can give you a fair start. But it cannot finish the race for you. Only you can do that.

The world is changing. In the next year, almost every writer will use some form of AI. That is not a threat to the craft. It is a call to raise the standard. We can publish more, and we can also publish better. We can make fewer mistakes, and we can also speak with more care. We can move faster, and we can also stay honest. The choice is ours.

If you remember only one thing, remember this. Your name is your signature. Protect it. Use tools, but do not hide behind them. Learn from them, but do not copy their voice. Be bold enough to sound like yourself. Be patient enough to check your facts. Be kind enough to think about the person on the other side of the page.

Thank you for reading this book. It was made to be the spine you lean on when the process feels heavy, and the map you follow when the path feels unclear. Use it to plan your next chapter, your next article, or your next book. Use it to recover your voice when you lose it. Use it to teach others who are just starting out.

Write with courage. Edit with care. Publish with integrity. If you do, your work will carry light. It will help someone breathe easier, think deeper, or try again. That is the real measure of a writer. That is the work that lasts. Love you all. I will catch you on the other side.

POP

19

Final Chapter: Patience, Passes, and the Real Partnership

Everything in this book leads here. Writing with ChatGPT is not about tricks or shortcuts. It is about patience, rhythm, and partnership. The goal is not to make machines write for us. The goal is to learn how to guide them with care so that our work stays human, warm, and true.

Good writing takes time. You bring your ideas, your heart, and your purpose. ChatGPT brings speed, structure, and clarity. Together, you shape something better through patience and repetition.

Each project takes passes. Some chapters may need ten or more. Every pass matters because it brings you closer to balance. You teach ChatGPT your rhythm, and ChatGPT helps refine your words. The writers who grow the most are not the fastest. They are the ones who stay curious, keep reading, and keep adjusting until every line feels right.

Proofreading and Dictation

Proofreading is your mirror. Dictation is your voice. Reading your writing aloud helps you hear where it loses energy. Dictating directly into ChatGPT helps capture the rhythm of speech and emotion. Use your phone or computer to speak your ideas. Then say, "Keep my tone. Fix grammar only." This helps ChatGPT polish your text without removing your personality.

Working in Passes

Writing with ChatGPT happens in stages. Each mode is one pass. Together, these modes build accuracy, warmth, and credibility.

1. Humanize Mode: Makes your writing sound natural and removes stiffness.
2. Accuracy Mode: Checks every fact and flags details that need proof.
3. Objective Mode: Reads your work with balance and fairness.
4. Verification Mode: Confirms that each source or citation is real.
5. Continuity Mode: Keeps tone, style, and structure steady across your project.
6. Attribution Check: Makes sure that all borrowed ideas and quotes are credited.

You do not have to use every mode every time. Focus on what your project needs. Each pass builds confidence.

Fighting Synthetic Writing

Synthetic writing looks smooth but feels empty. It happens when people stop too early and publish the first draft that ChatGPT gives them. Do not do that. Ask ChatGPT for several versions of your paragraph or section. Compare them. Mix the best parts together. Add real examples or stories from your life. That is how your words become alive again.

The Impossible Em Dash Rule

There is no magic way to make ChatGPT stop using em dashes. They are built into the model's patterns. The fix is discipline. Each time you review a draft, say, "Remove all em dashes and use complete sentences." Then review again. If any remain, repeat the command. Over time, this becomes second nature. Precision grows with patience.

Building and Updating the Knowledge Base

Your Knowledge Base is what keeps ChatGPT consistent. Upload your outlines, research notes, and facts. This gives ChatGPT context so it does not guess or forget.

Re-upload often. After every few chapters or major edits, upload the latest version of your book or project. Ask ChatGPT to export a clean doc file of your progress. Save it. Then re-upload it to refresh memory. This stops errors and keeps the model aligned with your vision.

Keep five files in your Knowledge Base:

- Facts Ledger: Verified information, with sources and dates.
- Glossary: Key terms and definitions.
- Decisions Log: Notes about voice, tone, and creative direction.
- Outline Versions: Every version of your outline in order.
- Citations Database: All references in APA format.

Start each new session by pasting your updated outline and Glossary. End each session by updating your files. These small steps build long-term consistency.

The Real Workflow

Here is the process that works:

1. Dictate your idea directly into ChatGPT.
2. Ask ChatGPT to clean grammar while keeping your tone.
3. Create a short outline that protects your message.
4. Write in full paragraphs. No lists or fragments.
5. Run Humanize Mode to smooth tone.
6. Run Accuracy Mode and Verification Mode to confirm facts.
7. Run Objective Mode for balance and logic.
8. Remove all em dashes and check punctuation.
9. Run Attribution Check for citations.
10. Export your progress to a doc file and re-upload it to your Knowledge Base.

Each step strengthens your writing and builds a clean workflow.

The Patience Factor

Many writers lose patience after the first few drafts. They publish too soon and end up with mechanical or shallow work. Great writing takes feedback and time. Every new pass makes your voice sharper.

This process is not about perfection. It is about partnership. ChatGPT listens, adjusts, and learns your rhythm as you guide it. Over time, this back-and-forth makes both of you better.

Readers care about truth and emotion. They want to feel your voice behind every word. When your writing is careful, accurate, and human, they can tell.

The goal is not to write fast. The goal is to write right. Using ChatGPT with discipline helps you find balance between speed and authenticity. Dictate, refine, re-upload, and repeat. That is the path to your best work.

ChatGPT is your partner, not your replacement. Use it to think faster, edit cleaner, and protect your truth. With patience, practice, and structure, you can create writing that sounds like no one else's.

Final Recap

- Dictation captures rhythm and tone.
- Passes build quality through patience.
- Knowledge Base uploads prevent memory loss.
- Removing em dashes protects flow and clarity.
- Modes help refine tone, facts, and ethics.
- You remain the author. ChatGPT is the tool.

Thank you for caring about the craft of writing. If you are reading this, you already value clarity, truth, and the power of your own voice. ChatGPT is here to help you write faster and polish your ideas, but only you can make the words real. Keep creating. Keep refining. Keep sounding like you.

www.ingramcontent.com/pod-product-compliance
Ingram Content Group UK Ltd.
Pitfield, Milton Keynes, MK11 3LW, UK
UKHW010008031026
15589UKWH00008B/1527